W9-BAI-186

Explore the Universe

OBSERVATORIES IN SPACE

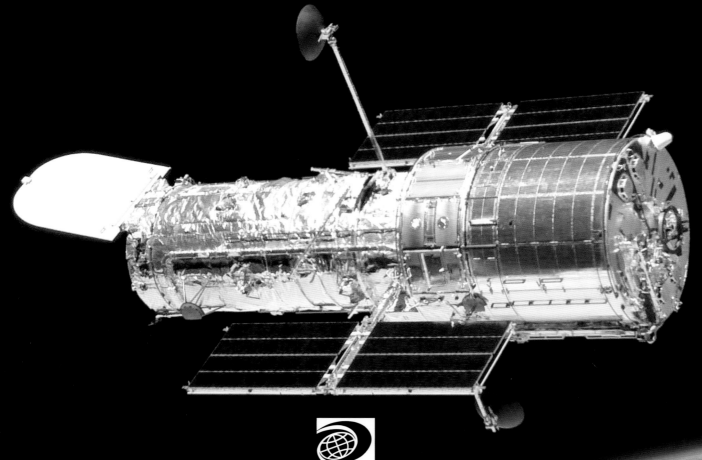

![WORLD BOOK logo]

WORLD
BOOK

a Scott Fetzer company
Chicago
www.worldbookonline.com

World Book, Inc.
233 N. Michigan Avenue
Chicago, IL 60601
U.S.A.

For information about other World Book publications, visit our
Web site at **http://www.worldbookonline.com** or call
1-800-WORLDBK (967-5325).

For information about sales to schools and
libraries, call **1-800-975-3250 (United States)**,
or **1-800-837-5365 (Canada)**.

Library of Congress Cataloging-in-Publication data
Observatories in space.
     p. cm. -- (Explore the universe)
     Summary: "An introduction to observatories in space with
information about their history and use. Includes diagrams,
fun facts, glossary, resource list and index"--Provided by
publisher.
     Includes index.
     ISBN 978-0-7166-9554-7
     1. Astronomical observatories--Juvenile literature.
     2. Astronomical instruments--Juvenile literature.
     I. World Book, Inc.
     QB81.O266 2010
     522'.2919--dc22
                                    2009040316

ISBN 978-0-7166-9544-8 (set)
Printed in China by Leo Paper Products, LTD.,
Heshan, Guangdong
1st printing February 2010

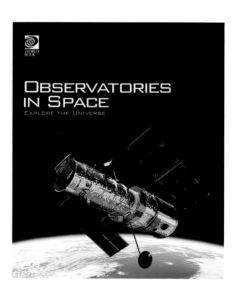

Cover image:
The Hubble Space
Telescope, launched in
1990, is one of the most
important scientific
instruments ever
created. The Hubble
has given scientists
unprecedented views of
the solar system and
beyond, revolutionizing
our understanding of
the cosmos.

European Space Agency

CONTENTS

Introduction 4

Why do astronomers need observatories in air and in space? 6

FOCUS ON: Balloon Observatories 8

What is an airborne observatory? 10

What are sounding rockets? 12

What are space probes? 14

What is an orbiting observatory? 16

What were the first observatories in space? .18

How does an observatory get into space? 20

What are the parts of an orbiting observatory? 22

FOCUS ON: The Electromagnetic Spectrum 24

What can astronomers learn by studying light from space? 26

What is the Hubble Space Telescope? 28

FOCUS ON: Hubble's View of the Universe .30

Are radio telescopes used in space? 32

How does an infrared telescope work? 34

How do scientists use orbiting infrared telescopes? 36

How does an ultraviolet telescope work? 38

How do scientists use orbiting ultraviolet telescopes? 40

How does an X-ray telescope work? 42

How do scientists use orbiting X-ray telescopes? 44

How is a gamma-ray telescope unique? 46

What have orbiting gamma-ray telescopes revealed about
gamma-ray bursts? 48

Can orbiting observatories be used to study deep space? 50

Can orbiting observatories be used to study Earth? 52

Can orbiting observatories be used to study the sun? 54

Can orbiting observatories be used to search for extrasolar planets? 56

What does the future hold for space-based observatories? 58

Glossary 60

For more information 62

Index 63

Acknowledgments 64

If a word is printed in **bold letters that look like this,** that word's meaning is given in the glossary on pages 60-61.

INTRODUCTION

For thousands of years, people have studied the heavens. Some of the first stone buildings were dedicated to observing the stars. Over the centuries, new technology led to great improvements in astronomy, forever changing our view of the universe.

However, there are limitations to studying the heavens from the ground. Earth's atmosphere blurs images. It also blocks certain kinds of light. Today, many exciting astronomical discoveries are being made by observatories orbiting in space. By leaving the atmosphere behind, scientists have launched a new age in astronomy.

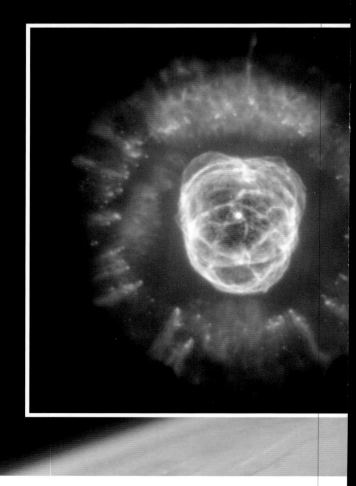

The Hubble Space Telescope, launched in 1990, revolutionized astronomy with images of unprecedented detail. The Hubble has given us exquisite views of many new as well as well-known objects, including the beautiful Eskimo Nebula (left).

BIRTH OF A TWINKLE

A clear night sky is filled with twinkling **stars.** Yet, stars do not actually twinkle at all. The light from stars only appears to change because of **atmospheric distortion.** Atmospheric distortion affects how our eyes—and the **lenses** and mirrors of telescopes—see stars.

Twinkles are ultimately caused by the sun, whose energy warms the gases in Earth's atmosphere. The sun does not warm the gases evenly, however. This unevenness creates moving pockets of air that act like lenses by bending incoming light. For astronomers to obtain a clear image from a telescope, light rays from a celestial object must all come to a focus at one point. But the air pockets in the atmosphere *distort* (bend) the light rays, causing them to strike a telescope lens or mirror at many points. The result is a blurry image.

HEAVY BLANKET

In addition to distorting light rays, the atmosphere blocks certain kinds of light. The light that people see, called **visible light,** is only one part of the entire range of **electromagnetic radiation.** Light rays that are more energetic or less energetic than visible light can tell astronomers much about the universe. But the atmosphere blocks all or most of these forms of light like a heavy blanket. To observe such light, astronomers must lift their instruments above the atmosphere.

THIN AIR

The simplest way to escape the atmosphere is to climb a mountain. At higher elevations, the atmosphere grows thinner, which reduces atmospheric distortion. As a result, many **observatories** have been built on mountains.

To climb higher still, astronomers attach telescopes to special balloons that rise through the atmosphere. Airplanes traveling at high altitudes can act as airborne observatories. The ultimate escape is outer space. Today, astronomers have sent dozens of observatories into space, completely beyond the atmosphere.

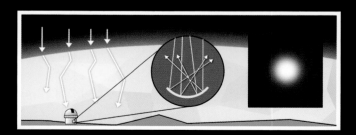

Moving pockets of air act like lenses in the atmosphere, causing light rays to cross at many points (center).

Such atmospheric distortion can blur the images taken by telescopes on the ground.

Earth's atmosphere causes many optical telescopes on Earth to produce blurry images. In addition, the atmosphere blocks certain types of light invisible to human eyes.

A cloud of dust and gas that blocks a view of stars forming in a nebula becomes transparent in an image taken in *infrared light* (heat radiation) by the Spitzer Space Telescope. This region is home to more than 2,200 stars.

Lightwaves that reach observatories in space remain parallel because they do not pass through the atmosphere.

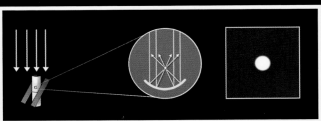

The parallel light waves bounce back to a single point (center), producing a tightly focused image.

BALLOON OBSERVATORIES

One of the earliest ways that astronomers lifted their instruments above the atmosphere was by using special balloons. Even in this age of advanced space telescopes, astronomers continue to use balloons, which are relatively affordable and can be launched quickly. Balloons can achieve altitudes of 20 miles (32 kilometers) or more and remain aloft for weeks. They can carry scientific instruments weighing 2 tons (1,800 kilograms) or more. As the largest of these balloons climb, they slowly expand to the size of a sports stadium.

A balloon launched in Sweden carries instruments for observing the sun and its magnetic field.

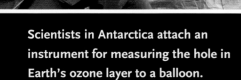

Scientists in Antarctica attach an instrument for measuring the hole in Earth's ozone layer to a balloon.

An observation balloon costs only a fraction of the cost of a rocket.

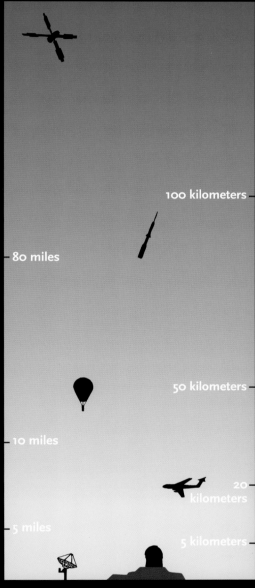

100 kilometers

80 miles

50 kilometers

10 miles

20 kilometers

5 miles

5 kilometers

A variety of technologies, including planes, balloons, sounding rockets, and satellites, are used to carry scientific instruments aloft. Because the atmosphere thins with altitude, even small increases in height above Earth's surface can improve the quality of images captured by airborne instruments.

For many observations, it is not necessary to completely escape the atmosphere. An airplane at high altitude flies above most of Earth's atmosphere.

INFRARED IN THE WILD BLUE YONDER

Airborne **observatories** are especially useful for observing **infrared light,** or heat radiation. Infrared is invisible to people but can be observed by telescopes. Although some infrared light reaches the Earth's surface, water vapor and gases in the lower atmosphere absorb most of it. By fitting high-flying airborne observatories with infrared telescopes, astronomers have made many important discoveries.

WINDOW GLASS AND OXYGEN MASKS

The National Aeronautics and Space Administration (NASA) built the first airborne observatory in the 1960's. The observatory, called Galileo, carried infrared telescopes. Unfortunately, the telescopes had to be pointed through the glass in the observatory's windows, and the glass blocked much of the infrared light. Nevertheless, astronomers using Galileo discovered water ice in Saturn's rings. They also found that the clouds above Venus do not contain water vapor.

In 1967, NASA scientists removed a window from another airborne observatory. For the first time, astronomers could see inside the interstellar clouds of dust and gas in our **galaxy.** However, removing the window caused other problems. The advantage of flying at high altitude is that the air is thin. Unfortunately, the open window exposed astronomers to this thin air, forcing them to wear oxygen masks to breathe. This requirement complicated observations.

Astronomers aboard NASA's Kuiper Airborne Observatory (left), the first major airborne astronomical observatory, made numerous discoveries, including finding rings around Uranus and water in Jupiter's atmosphere. Kuiper flew more than 1,400 missions from 1975 to 1995.

UP AND AWAY

In 1974, NASA completed the Kuiper Airborne Observatory, which carried a 36-inch (91.5-centimeter) infrared telescope. Engineers cut an opening in the plane body for the telescope and sealed it off from the rest of the plane, eliminating the need for masks. Among other findings, Kuiper discovered rings around the **planet** Uranus and observed **stars** forming.

THE SKY IS THE LIMIT

By 2010, NASA expected to fly a new observatory, the Stratospheric Observatory for Infrared Astronomy (SOFIA). SOFIA is a Boeing 747 jumbo jet fitted with an 8-foot (2.5-meter) infrared telescope. The plane has a huge opening in its side for the largest telescope ever mounted in an airborne observatory.

Scientists study information collected by SOFIA's *infrared* (heat) telescope during a test.

The 8-foot (2.5-meter) mirror in NASA's Stratospheric Observatory for Infrared Astronomy (SOFIA) is removed for servicing. The mirror is by far the largest ever carried by an aircraft.

To lift instruments above Earth's upper atmosphere, astronomers use **sounding rockets** as well as balloons. Most sounding rockets are relatively small rockets that do not go high enough to reach orbit—about 100 miles (160 kilometers) above Earth. Sounding rockets travel upward and then back down in a curved path called a trajectory. They carry instruments above Earth's atmosphere for periods lasting about 15 minutes.

ANATOMY OF A ROCKET

The basic parts of a sounding rocket include the fuel, the chamber, the nozzle, and the **payload.** In astronomical sounding rockets, the payload consists of instruments used to make observations.

As a rocket burns fuel in the chamber, it produces hot gases that rush out of the nozzle. The force created by the escaping gases pushes the rocket upward.

DID YOU KNOW?

In the 1200's A.D., the Chinese invented the first solid-fuel rocket engine, a tube filled with gunpowder.

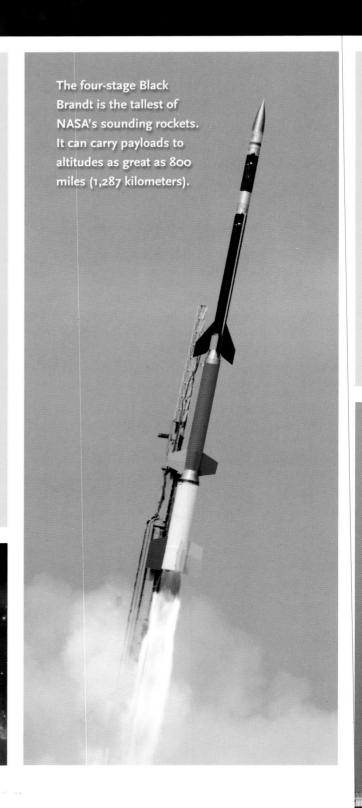

The four-stage Black Brandt is the tallest of NASA's sounding rockets. It can carry payloads to altitudes as great as 800 miles (1,287 kilometers).

X-RAY GLOW

The first observations of **X rays** from deep space were made using a sounding rocket. In 1962, scientists launched a rocket that carried a Geiger counter, an instrument that detects X rays. X rays are blocked by the upper atmosphere, so sounding rockets gave scientists their first good chance to observe this kind of light.

Astronomers knew the sun gave off X rays, but the 1962 flight revealed Scorpius X-1, the brightest source of X rays outside the solar system. Astronomers also learned that the universe is filled with a background glow of X rays.

ROCKET ON

Although satellite observatories have largely replaced sounding rockets, the rockets are still useful. They are relatively cheap, and scientists can launch them quickly. If scientists detect an exploding star, they can quickly launch astronomical equipment with sounding rockets to make observations. Astronomers also use the rockets to test equipment and to train astronomy students.

An Orion sounding rocket blasts off with a payload designed by students from several universities in Virginia.

Sounding rockets are smaller versions of the rockets used to carry vehicles and scientific instruments into Earth orbit and beyond.

ON THE FLY

Some **space probes** fly past celestial objects. In 1959, both the United States and the Soviet Union (now Russia) sent space probes to orbit the moon. The craft carried cameras to take pictures of the surface. By 1966, U.S. and Soviet probes began to land on the moon.

In the 1960's, scientists sent space probes to the inner, rocky **planets** of the **solar system,** namely Mercury, Venus, and Mars. In the 1970's, scientists launched the Pioneer and Voyager probes, which flew by the gas-giant planets Jupiter, Saturn, Uranus, and Neptune. In 2006, NASA launched New Horizons, which will fly by Pluto in 2015.

Astronomers have also sent probes to several **comets** and **asteroids.** Most of these probes were fly-bys that took close-up pictures. In 2004, a probe collected dust from a comet's tail. In 2005, a probe crashed into a comet while a fly-by probe analyzed material from the collision to learn which materials made up the comet.

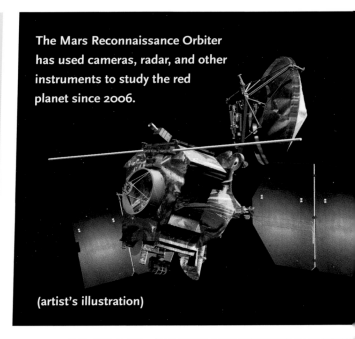

The Mars Reconnaissance Orbiter has used cameras, radar, and other instruments to study the red planet since 2006.

(artist's illustration)

DID YOU KNOW?

On Feb. 17, 1998, the Voyager 1 space probe became the most remote human-made object in space. By 2009, the probe was about 10 billion miles (16 billion kilometers) from the sun.

The Huygens probe landed on Saturn's moon Titan in 2005, giving scientists their first view of the surface of this exotic, cloud-covered moon.

(artist's illustration)

ATMOSPHERIC PROBES AND LANDERS

Space probes can also drop atmospheric probes and landers. Atmospheric probes drop slowly by parachute, making observations as they fall through the atmosphere. For example, in 1995, the Galileo space probe dropped a smaller probe into the atmosphere of Jupiter. In 2005, the Cassini spacecraft released the Huygens probe into the atmosphere of Titan, Saturn's largest moon. The surface of Titan is covered in thick clouds, so only a probe could explore it.

Space probes have also dropped landers to the surface of Mars, the moon, and Venus. The NASA rovers Spirit and Opportunity reached Mars in 2004, to spend years sampling rocks and taking photographs. In 2008, the Phoenix lander confirmed that there is water ice on Mars. Water is essential to life on Earth, so scientists wonder whether life might develop on other planets with water.

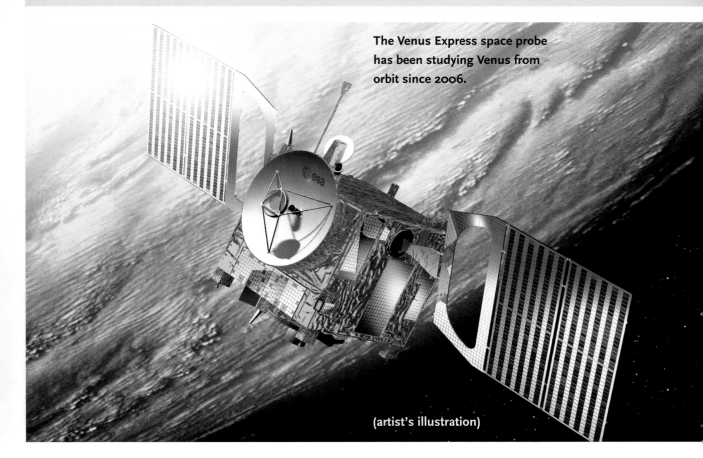

The Venus Express space probe has been studying Venus from orbit since 2006.

(artist's illustration)

Airplanes and **sounding rockets** provided astronomers with their first observations made above the atmosphere. However, brief trips above the atmosphere do not allow for the long-term studies astronomers can make with ground-based **observatories.** In order for space-based astronomy to realize its full potential, scientists had to launch observatories into orbit.

DELICATE BALANCE

The orbit of a space-based observatory is the curved path it takes around the Earth. An orbit represents a delicate balance between **gravity** and *velocity* (speed in a certain direction). The gravity of Earth prevents the observatory from escaping into space. At the same time, the observatory must travel fast enough to keep gravity from pulling it back down to Earth. The speeds required are impressive. Some observatories travel at more than 15,000 miles (25,000 kilometers) per hour. Only powerful rockets can accelerate observatories to such speeds. An observatory may orbit indefinitely, as long as it maintains its velocity.

Infrared images taken by the Herschel Space Observatory are especially useful for seeing through clouds of dust and gas in deep space.

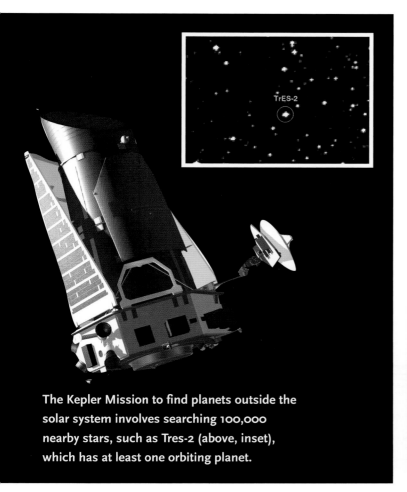

The Kepler Mission to find planets outside the solar system involves searching 100,000 nearby stars, such as Tres-2 (above, inset), which has at least one orbiting planet.

The Herschel spacecraft observes in infrared light, enabling it to image star formation in distant galaxies (right).

ORBITAL REAL ESTATE

The orbits of some observatories are almost circular. The orbits of others are in the shape of an *ellipse* (oval). Orbits can be as low as 155 miles (250 kilometers) or more than 20,000 miles (32,200 kilometers) above Earth. An orbit may keep an observatory over the same spot above Earth in a so-called geostationary orbit, or it may circle the globe in little more than an hour.

UNDER THE HOOD

Orbiting observatories carry many different kinds of telescopes. The Hubble Space Telescope observes **visible light,** along with some **infrared light** and **ultraviolet light.** The Herschel Space Observatory observes infrared light. The Fermi Gamma-ray Space Telescope observes **gamma rays.**

The space age began when the Soviet Union (now Russia) launched the first artificial satellite into orbit in 1957. The satellite was called Sputnik. Although it carried out certain measurements of the upper atmosphere, Sputnik had only limited capabilities. In 1958, the United States launched the satellite Explorer 1, which detected belts of radiation around the Earth that became known as the Van Allen belts.

ARIEL

The first true space-based **observatories** were the Ariel satellites built by the United Kingdom and the United States. The first Ariel satellite was launched in 1962. It studied **ultraviolet** and **X-ray** radiation given off by the sun. Later Ariel satellites observed **radio waves** and studied Earth's upper atmosphere. However, the Ariel satellites were relatively small and did not remain in orbit for long.

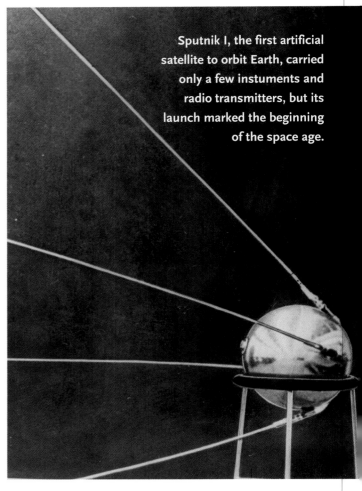

Sputnik I, the first artificial satellite to orbit Earth, carried only a few instuments and radio transmitters, but its launch marked the beginning of the space age.

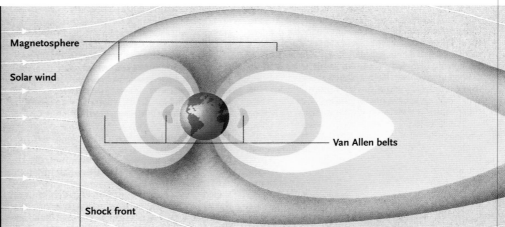

Explorer 1, the first artificial satellite launched by the United States, detected the Van Allen belts, two zones of electrically charged particles that surround Earth high above its surface.

Magnetosphere

Solar wind

Van Allen belts

Shock front

The space age began with the launch in 1957 of the first artificial satellite, Sputnik I. The first large orbiting astronomical observatory was launched in 1968.

ULTRAVIOLET PIONEER

Space-based astronomy came into its own with the Orbiting Astronomical Observatory-2 (OAO-2), launched by the United States in 1968. OAO-2 was one of a series of four orbiting observatories launched by NASA between 1966 and 1972. These observatories were large, powerful, and long lasting.

OAO-2 carried telescopes that observed more than 1,200 celestial bodies in ultraviolet light for the first time, including **planets, comets, stars,** and **galaxies.** OAO-2 also allowed astronomers to study ultraviolet light given off by exploding stars called **supernovae.** Supernovae may produce millions or even billions of times as much **electromagnetic radiation** as the sun.

THE EINSTEIN OBSERVATORY

In 1977, NASA launched the first of three High Energy Astronomy Observatory (HEAO) satellites. These were the largest observatories yet, weighing about 3 tons (2,700 kilograms) each. These observatories studied X rays and **gamma rays.** The Einstein Observatory, or HEAO 2, carried an X-ray telescope that was hundreds of times more sensitive than any previously launched.

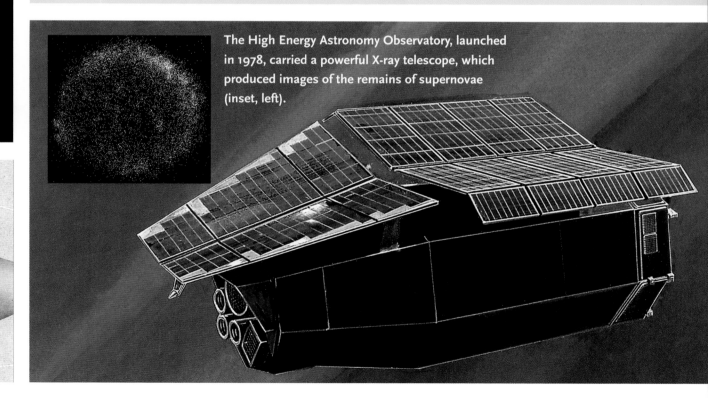

The High Energy Astronomy Observatory, launched in 1978, carried a powerful X-ray telescope, which produced images of the remains of supernovae (inset, left).

Space-based **observatories** need the power of rocket engines to escape the pull of Earth's **gravity.** As observatories have become larger and heavier, they have needed more powerful rockets to reach orbit.

POWER AND WEIGHT

When the space age began, rockets were relatively weak, which limited the amount of **payload** they could carry. In astronomy, a payload consists of the scientific instruments carried by the rocket. The first U.S. satellite, Explorer 1, weighed only 17 pounds (8 kilograms). However, rockets soon became more powerful, allowing for heavier payloads. By 1968, NASA was able to launch the 4,400-pound (2,000-kilogram) OAO-2 observatory into orbit. In 1991, the space shuttle Discovery lifted the Compton Gamma Ray Observatory into orbit. This observatory was 70 feet (21.3 meters) long and weighed more than 38,000 pounds (17,000 kilograms).

The first United States satellite, Explorer I, blasts into space on Jan. 31, 1958, atop a modified Jupiter C rocket. The launch of the satellite, which weighed only 17 pounds (8 kilograms), marked the U.S. entry into the space age.

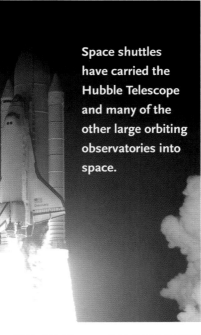

Space shuttles have carried the Hubble Telescope and many of the other large orbiting observatories into space.

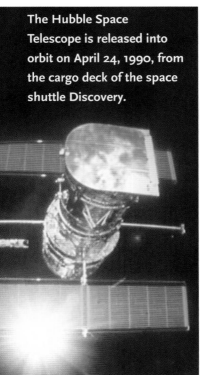

The Hubble Space Telescope is released into orbit on April 24, 1990, from the cargo deck of the space shuttle Discovery.

LAUNCH VEHICLES

Most observatories are launched into orbit using unpiloted rockets made of a number of sections called stages. A rocket must lift not only the payload but also the weight of the rocket itself. By dumping stages that have used up all their fuel, multistage rockets are able to make the most of their remaining fuel.

Many of the largest observatories, including the Hubble Space Telescope, were carried into orbit by one of the space shuttles. The space shuttle has booster rockets and a fuel tank that fall away after use. This arrangement allows the shuttle to carry as much as 50,000 pounds (22,700 kilograms) of cargo into orbit.

The most powerful rocket developed by NASA was the Saturn V, which could carry 260,000 pounds (118,000 kilograms) into orbit. However, NASA has plans to build a rocket that would shatter the old record. The Ares V will lift about 410,000 pounds (188,000 kilograms) into orbit. That's the weight of 16 school buses. Like the space shuttle, the Ares V will use booster rockets. It could launch as early as 2019.

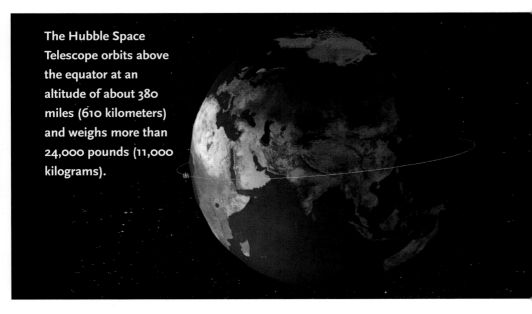

The Hubble Space Telescope orbits above the equator at an altitude of about 380 miles (610 kilometers) and weighs more than 24,000 pounds (11,000 kilograms).

WHAT ARE THE PARTS OF AN ORBITING OBSERVATORY?

THE EYES

Telescopes form the heart of any **observatory.** Different types of telescopes observe different forms of **electromagnetic radiation.** Most telescopes use mirrors to gather and focus light. These telescopes record images using a special kind of computer chip called a **charge-coupled device (CCD).** CCD's are more sensitive to light than any kind of photographic film. Computers on board the observatory record information collected by the CCD.

Observatories may also house other equipment. For example, an instrument called a **spectrometer** can tell astronomers which chemicals are in a **star** or other celestial body.

NO WALL SOCKETS

All this equipment needs electric power to operate, but there are no wall sockets in space. Orbiting observatories generate electric power using **solar panels.** Solar panels are able to convert light from the sun into electric energy. The solar panels unfold like sails after the observatory goes into orbit. Solar panels charge batteries that provide power when the observatory is in Earth's shadow.

Scientists prepare the Herschel Space Observatory for launch in 2009. The telescope's 138-inch (3.5-meter) mirror is the largest yet launched into space.

In addition to telescopes and other instruments, an orbiting observatory must carry equipment to provide power for the observatory and for communicating with Earth.

PHONING HOME

Orbiting observatories send large amounts of data back to astronomers on the ground using special radio antennas. For example, every week the Hubble Space Telescope transmits back data that are equal to 3,600 feet (1,100 meters) of books on a shelf. Radio receivers also pick up commands from ground control. Radio comman the ground can direct small rockets satellite to move an observatory into higher orbit or to change the directio which the telescopes point. Other de hold the observatory steady as it crea images.

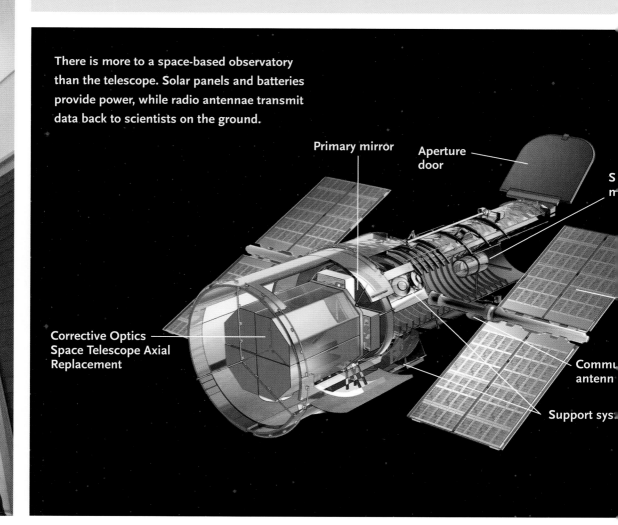

There is more to a space-based observatory than the telescope. Solar panels and batteries provide power, while radio antennae transmit data back to scientists on the ground.

Primary mirror

Aperture door

S
m

Corrective Optics
Space Telescope Axial
Replacement

Commu
antenn

Support sys

THE ELECTROMAGNETIC SPECTRUM

The sunlight that shines down on us on a summer day represents only a small part of the *spectrum* (range) of electromagnetic radiation. Human beings can only see visible light, though certain other animals can also see infrared or ultraviolet light. There is no fundamental difference between the different parts of the electromagnetic spectrum. From radio waves to gamma rays, all are forms of light. What distinguishes these forms is their wavelengths, or the distance between peaks in the waves that make up light. Forms of light also differ in their energy. Radio waves have the longest wavelengths and the lowest energy, and gamma rays have the shortest wavelengths and the highest energy. The universe is filled with every kind of light, so astronomers study the full spectrum, much of it from space.

Astronomers can learn about a star's motion by analyzing the light it gives off. If a star's light is shifted toward the red end of the spectrum, the star is moving away from Earth. If the light is shifted toward the blue end of the spectrum, the star is moving toward us.

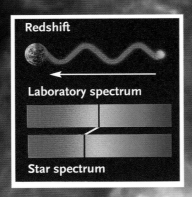

Redshift

Laboratory spectrum

Star spectrum

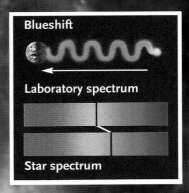

Blueshift

Laboratory spectrum

Star spectrum

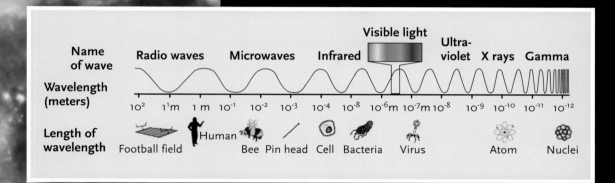

Name of wave	Radio waves	Microwaves	Infrared	Visible light	Ultra-violet	X rays	Gamma
Wavelength (meters)	10^2 1^1m 1 m 10^{-1}	10^{-2} 10^{-3}	10^{-4} 10^{-8} $10^{-6}m$ $10^{-7}m$ 10^{-8}		10^{-9}	10^{-10} 10^{-11}	10^{-12}
Length of wavelength	Football field	Human Bee Pin head	Cell Bacteria Virus			Atom	Nuclei

◄ A previously unknown network of cold gas clouds bursting with newborn stars (red in background image) threads through the dense central plane of the Milky Way in a false-color image made by the Herschel Space Observatory in 2009. The Herschel's infrared (heat-sensing) telescopes revealed the stellar nurseries, which are surrounded by dust that blocks visible light. In the false-color image, different colors represent different wavelengths of infrared light, with red indicating the coldest material.

▲
Different forms of electromagnetic energy have different wavelengths. The longest waves, radio waves, can be as long as a sports field. Infrared light has wavelengths as long as a human cell. The wavelengths of ultraviolet light are shorter than the viruses that cause colds. X rays have wavelengths as short as a single atom. Finally, gamma rays have wavelengths as tiny as the *nucleus* (core) of an atom.

Light is an electromagnetic wave. It consists of electric and magnetic fields that vary in a regular cycle at right angles to each other and to the direction of the wave's travel. The amplitude represents the largest value of each field.

▼

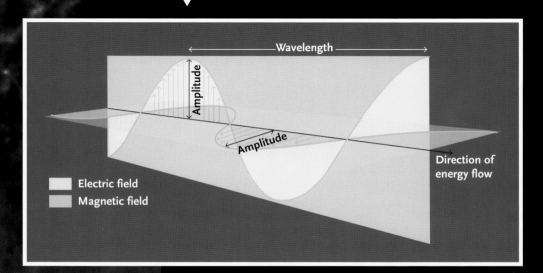

Light from the sun may appear white to us, but it is really made up of a rainbow of colors called the **spectrum.** The colors of **visible light** range from red to violet. Beyond red is **infrared light,** which has a wavelength too long for people to see. Beyond violet is **ultraviolet light,** which has a wavelength too short for people to see.

TASTE THE STARS

Most observatories include a device called a **spectrometer.** A spectrometer divides light into a spectrum and records it for analysis. Every **chemical element** produces a unique pattern of lines in the spectrum. By studying these lines, astronomers can tell which elements make up distant **stars.**

STARS IN MOTION

The spectrum also reveals information about a star's motion. When a star is moving away from us, its light is stretched toward the

In 1704, Sir Isaac Newton proved that white light is made up of all the colors of the rainbow.

DID YOU KNOW?

The Kuiper Airborne Observatory, the first major airborne astronomical observatory, was named for American astronomer Gerard P. Kuiper. The disk of comets distantly orbiting the sun also was named the Kuiper belt in his honor.

Chemical elements produce unique patterns of lines in the spectrum that astronomers can detect in light.

Hydrogen

Oxygen

longer, red **wavelengths.** When it is moving toward us, the light is pressed toward the shorter, blue wavelengths. This shift in wavelength is called the **Doppler effect.**

COSMOLOGICAL REDSHIFT

Light that travels a great distance also shows shifted wavelength. This shift is not caused by the movement of stars but by the expansion of space itself.

Scientists believe that the universe began about 13.7 billion years ago in an explosion called the **big bang.** Since the big bang, the universe has expanded from a single point to its present size. As the universe expands, it stretches the light traveling through space. This stretching is called cosmological **redshift.**

By measuring cosmological redshift, astronomers can tell how far light has traveled. Light from the most distant **galaxies** shows the strongest redshift. Visible light traveling from distant galaxies is stretched so much that it arrives as longer infrared light or **radio waves.** Light from such galaxies has traveled for more than 13 billion years.

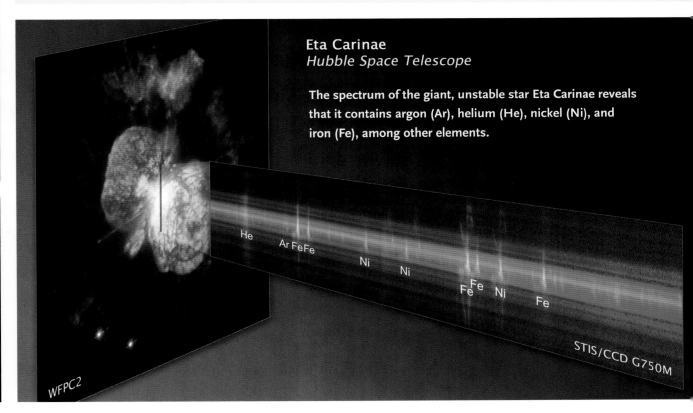

Eta Carinae
Hubble Space Telescope

The spectrum of the giant, unstable star Eta Carinae reveals that it contains argon (Ar), helium (He), nickel (Ni), and iron (Fe), among other elements.

The Hubble Space Telescope is one of the most important scientific instruments ever built. It has observed **planets** in the **solar system,** the birth and death of **stars,** and the distant reaches of the universe.

FUNHOUSE MIRROR

The heart of the Hubble is a telescope with a 94-inch (2.4-meter) mirror. The mirror collects **visible light, infrared light,** and **ultraviolet light**.

Shortly after Hubble was launched in 1990, astronomers discovered that the mirror was flawed. This flaw greatly reduced the quality of the telescope's images. Fortunately, astronauts repaired the telescope in 1993, reaching the telescope's 380-mile (610-kilometer) orbit in the space shuttle Endeavour. Astronauts have visited the telescope four times altogether, most recently in 2009. By repairing parts and upgrading equipment, scientists expect Hubble to operate through 2014. At that time, a more powerful telescope will take its place.

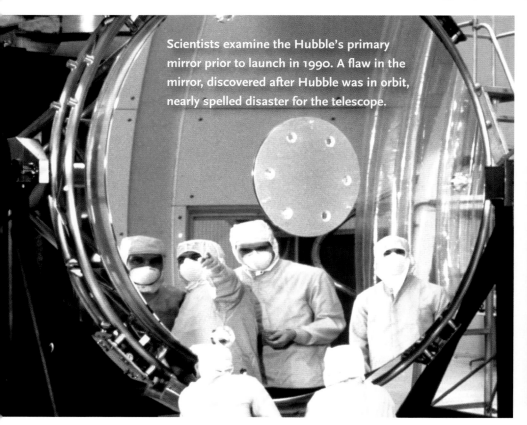

Scientists examine the Hubble's primary mirror prior to launch in 1990. A flaw in the mirror, discovered after Hubble was in orbit, nearly spelled disaster for the telescope.

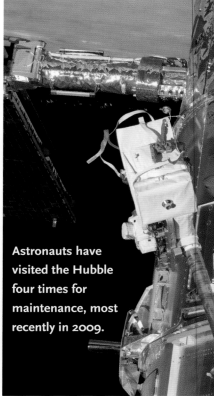

Astronauts have visited the Hubble four times for maintenance, most recently in 2009.

Scientists control the Hubble from the Space Telescope Science Institute in Baltimore, Maryland.

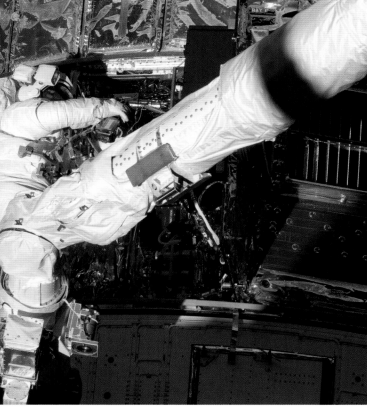

COSMIC SUPERSTAR

Despite its shaky beginning, Hubble went on to make phenomenal discoveries. It has produced the most detailed **optical** images ever recorded of objects in deep space. It has made pictures of newborn stars, images of **galaxies** colliding and tearing each other apart, and evidence suggesting that most galaxies have a massive **black hole** in their center.

NUTS AND BOLTS

Hubble measures more than 43 feet (13 meters) long, about the size of a tractor-trailer truck. The telescope weighed 24,500 pounds (11,110 kilograms) at launch. Like other powerful telescopes, Hubble measures light with a computer chip called a **charge-coupled device** and records the data in computers. Hubble also contains **spectrometers,** enabling astronomers to analyze light's **spectrum.**

The **observatory** generates electric power with **solar panels,** storing electricity in batteries. The power operates radio communications, devices that hold the observatory steady, and machinery for turning and pointing the telescope. The telescope is controlled by radio commands issued by scientists at the Space Telescope Science Institute in Baltimore, Maryland. Scientists around the world use the Hubble to expand our knowledge of the universe.

HUBBLE'S VIEW OF THE UNIVERSE

The Hubble Space Telescope has provided unprecedented views of the universe, forever changing our understanding of the planets of the solar system, how stars are born and die, and the overall structure of the universe.

A star that has thrown off its outer atmosphere, creating a colorful nebula, is one of many spectacular images captured by Hubble.

The Hubble Deep Field (background photograph) is a revolutionary image that stretches to the edge of the visible universe. The Deep Field shows only a tiny part of the sky, equivalent to the size of a tennis ball seen at 330 feet (100 meters). Yet even such a small part of the sky is filled with galaxies, some billions of light-years away. The Hubble Deep Field emphasizes the vast, complex nature of the universe.

Hubble can observe *infrared light* (heat radiation), which passes through great clouds of dust and gas, to reveal newborn stars. Such stars form deep within nebulae, such as the Cone Nebula.

A false-color ultraviolet image of Saturn taken by Hubble reveals the bands of rotating gas that make up the planet's atmosphere.

Radio waves have the longest wavelengths of all light. These waves can be more than 1 mile (1.6 kilometers) long. Shorter radio waves are called microwaves. Radio telescopes resemble the satellite dishes used to receive television signals. Radio telescopes may be quite large. For example, the Arecibo radio telescope in Puerto Rico is 1,000 feet (305 meters) across. Scientists cannot yet launch such large dishes into space.

A VIRTUAL DISH

Although radio telescopes on the ground are large, scientists need still-larger dishes to improve resolution. Resolution, or resolving power, is a measure of the amount of light a telescope can gather. By linking radio telescopes, astronomers can make them act as one enormous dish with high resolution. These virtual dishes can be made even larger with radio telescopes in orbit. By combining ground-based dishes with a 26-foot (8-meter) Japanese dish in orbit, astronomers have created a virtual dish nearly four times as large as Earth.

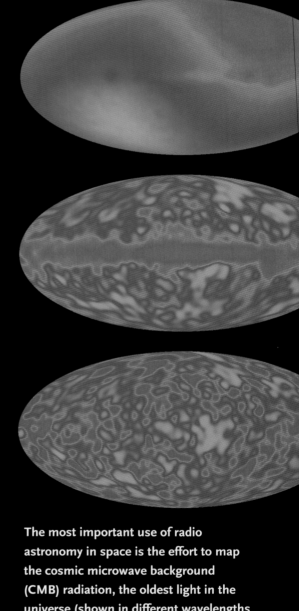

The most important use of radio astronomy in space is the effort to map the cosmic microwave background (CMB) radiation, the oldest light in the universe (shown in different wavelengths above).

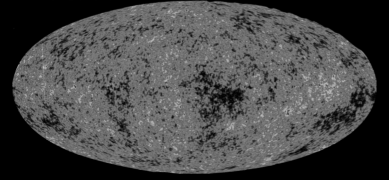

Variations in the CMB revealed by the Wilkinson Microwave Anisotropy Probe (WMAP) match the distribution of galaxies in the universe.

THE BIG AFTERGLOW

In the 1960's, astronomers discovered a faint hiss of microwaves coming from all over the universe. Scientists soon realized that this hiss was the afterglow of the **big bang.** In the beginning, the universe was filled with intense light. Billions of years later, the expansion of the universe has stretched the light into dim microwaves. Scientists call this afterglow the **cosmic microwave background (CMB) radiation.** It is the most ancient light that scientists can detect, and it provides clues to the structure of the universe itself.

As seen from orbit, the CMB shows tiny variations in different parts of the sky. These variations correspond with huge collections of galaxies, providing clues to how matter came together to form **stars** in the early universe. Astronomers have launched increasingly sensitive observatories to measure the CMB, including the Cosmic Background Explorer (COBE) and the Wilkinson Microwave Anisotropy Probe (WMAP). In 2009, scientists launched the Planck Space Observatory, the most sensitive observatory yet. To reduce interference by heat from the craft, the Planck is kept incredibly cold, at just one-tenth of a degree above absolute zero, which is about −459 °F (−273 °C).

A ribbon of the CMB radiation appears in one of the first images taken by the Planck Space Observatory, launched in 2009. It was scheduled to complete the most detailed map of the CMB ever created by 2012.

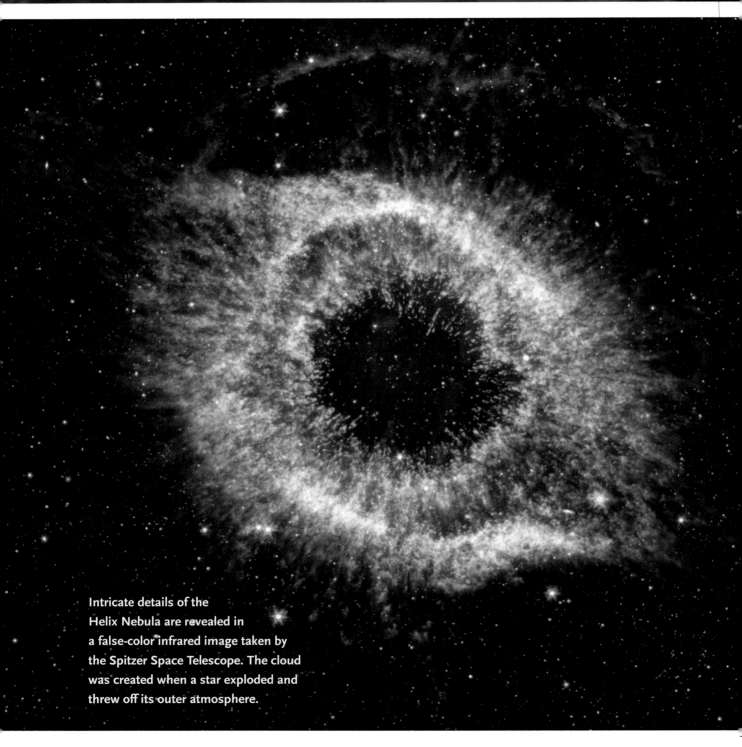

Intricate details of the Helix Nebula are revealed in a false-color infrared image taken by the Spitzer Space Telescope. The cloud was created when a star exploded and threw off its outer atmosphere.

Like **optical** telescopes, **infrared** telescopes collect and focus light using mirrors. Computer chips called **charge-coupled devices** record incoming infrared radiation and send the information to computers. The computers translate these data into images that we can see. However, infrared telescopes differ from optical telescopes in other respects.

RANGES OF THE INVISIBLE

Astronomers divide infrared light into three ranges called near-, mid-, and far-infrared. Telescopes on the ground can observe near-infrared. However, water vapor in Earth's atmosphere blocks out the other ranges of infrared. To observe mid- and far-infrared waves, **observatories** must escape Earth's atmosphere.

KEEPING COOL

Infrared radiation is heat radiation. Everything in the universe, including telescopes, gives off some infrared rays. In order to observe far-infrared waves, scientists must control "heat pollution" from the telescope itself. Astronomers use powerful coolants to keep infrared telescopes at low temperatures. For example, the Herschel Space Observatory uses liquid helium to keep its instruments at about −456 °F (−271 °C). That is near absolute zero, the lowest temperature scientists believe possible.

WET BLANKET

The first major infrared observatory, the Infrared Astronomical Satellite, was launched into orbit in 1983. However, NASA revolutionized infrared observations with the launch of the Spitzer Space Telescope in 2003. Coolant keeps the Spitzer cold, and a solar shield blocks heat from the sun.

In 2009, the European Space Agency (ESA) launched the Herschel Space Observatory, another infrared observatory. Herschel's 138-inch (3.5-meter) mirror is the largest ever launched into space. Like Spitzer, Herschel orbits the sun at a considerable distance from the Earth, about 930,000 miles (1.5 million kilometers) away. This distance reduces heat pollution from the planet.

Infrared astronomy is especially useful for observing areas, such as the core of the Milky Way, whose thick clouds of dust and gas block visible light.

HOW DO SCIENTISTS USE ORBITING INFRARED TELESCOPES?

THE INVISIBLE REVEALED

Infrared telescopes can detect heavenly bodies that are invisible to **optical** telescopes. Infrared is heat radiation, so even if a celestial body gives off no **visible light,** it may still glow in infrared light. The first infrared telescopes revealed countless objects that did not appear in visible light. These objects ranged from dying **stars** to clouds of debris around stars. Infrared telescopes have even observed **exoplanets,** or planets around other stars.

DUST BUSTER

Infrared telescopes have another advantage over optical telescopes. Thick clouds of dust and gas called **nebulae** may block visible light. Fortunately, much infrared light passes through nebulae. Infrared telescopes have discovered that many nebulae are stellar nurseries. Behind the veils of dust and gas, nebulae are giving birth to thousands of stars.

THE GALACTIC CORE

Infrared is also ideal for studying the center of our **galaxy,** which is obscured by thick clouds of dust and gas. Infrared telescopes have discovered that there are vast numbers of stars in the galaxy's core. Some of these stars are among the brightest, hottest stars in our galaxy.

BEYOND THE HORIZON

Infrared telescopes also enable astronomers to study the farthest reaches of the universe. **Redshift** stretches visible light from distant galaxies into infrared light. In 2008, infrared **observatories** discovered one of the most distant galaxies ever observed. Its light had traveled across more than 13 billion **light-years.**

An infrared image of the Andromeda Galaxy reveals a bright ring of newly forming stars that is hidden by dust in visible light.

In infrared light, a man's skin shines with heat, while a bottle of cold water appears dark.

Scientists use infrared telescopes to study stars being born in interstellar clouds of dust and gas. They also observe the center of our galaxy as well as distant galaxies.

Visible   Infrared

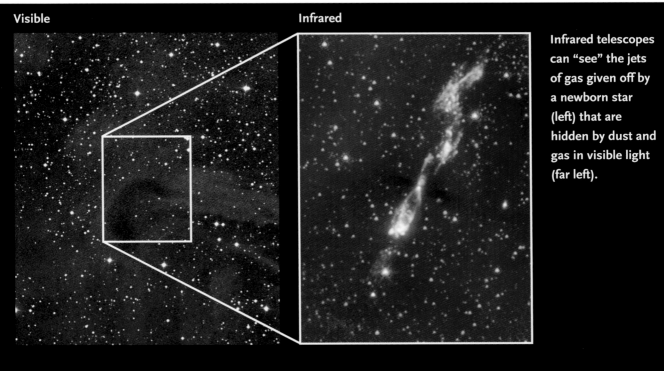

Infrared telescopes can "see" the jets of gas given off by a newborn star (left) that are hidden by dust and gas in visible light (far left).

Ultraviolet light, often called UV, is invisible to human eyes. It is called ultraviolet because it has shorter **wavelengths** than visible blue light. Some UV reaches the ground and causes suntans and sunburns. However, because most UV is blocked by Earth's atmosphere, most UV observations must be made from space.

VARIETIES OF ULTRAVIOLET

Most UV **observatories** contain telescopes with conventional mirrors. Scientists divide UV into three ranges: near, far, and extreme. Reflecting mirrors with special coatings can collect near and far UV light but not extreme UV. Many **optical** telescopes can observe near UV. For example, the Hubble Space Telescope carries a camera that takes pictures in the near ultraviolet range. Even telescopes that observe only UV may resemble an optical telescope, with mirrors focusing the ultraviolet image onto computer chips called **charge-coupled devices** that record the light.

Daisy petals that appear yellow (above) in visible light also have patterns that are revealed in ultraviolet light (below). Such patterns may help to guide bees, which can see in ultraviolet light, to the center of the flower.

DID YOU KNOW?

To escape Earth's gravity and enter orbit, a spacecraft must travel at a speed of 7 miles (11 kilometers) per second, about 25,000 miles (40,500 kilometers) per hour.

GOING TO EXTREMES

Extreme UV radiation has very short wavelengths. It is so energetic that it can pass straight through a reflecting mirror. Extreme UV will reflect from a mirror only if it strikes the mirror at a shallow angle. Extreme UV telescopes take advantage of this effect by using **grazing incidence mirrors.** These mirrors are arranged so that extreme UV will skip across their surface the the way a stone skips across the surface of a pond. Some grazing incidence mirrors are nested inside each other like tubes in an oil drum. The Extreme Ultraviolet Explorer, launched in 1992, carried grazing incidence mirrors.

ULTRAVIOLET SPECTROGRAPHS

Ultraviolet light is especially useful for exploring the **chemical elements** of heavenly bodies. Most UV observatories carry **spectrometers** that analyze the ultraviolet **spectrum.** These instruments reveal data that complement the data from optical spectrographs.

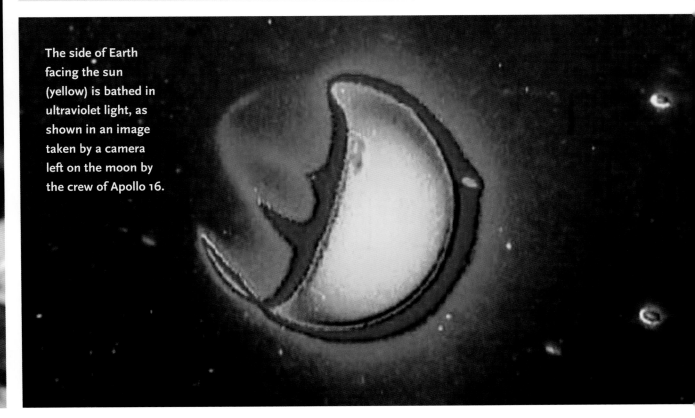

The side of Earth facing the sun (yellow) is bathed in ultraviolet light, as shown in an image taken by a camera left on the moon by the crew of Apollo 16.

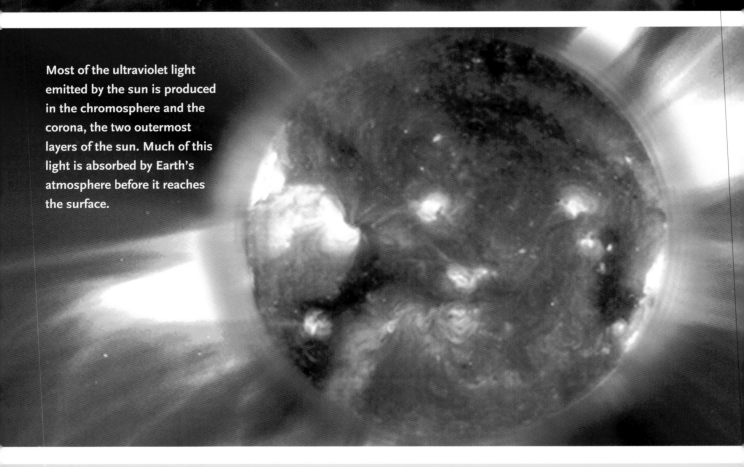

Most of the ultraviolet light emitted by the sun is produced in the chromosphere and the corona, the two outermost layers of the sun. Much of this light is absorbed by Earth's atmosphere before it reaches the surface.

Astronomers use **ultraviolet** telescopes to study heavenly bodies that are at high temperatures. Seen in ultraviolet light, the universe reveals exotic **stars** and violent events.

SOLAR STORMS

One source of UV light is close to home. The hot outer layer of the sun's atmosphere is called the **corona.** The corona reaches temperatures as high as 6 million Kelvin (10.8 million °F). At such temperatures, gas in the corona shines brightly in ultraviolet light. Astronomers have studied the sun's atmosphere using space **observatories** with ultraviolet telescopes. They have taken detailed images of solar flares, sudden bright spots on the sun's corona, and other solar storms. Scientists linked the powerful flares with "sunquakes," disturbances that ripple across the sun. UV telescopes can give warning if these storms will affect the Earth. The Hinode spacecraft launched in 2006 continues this research.

VIOLENT EVENTS

Ultraviolet telescopes observe some of the most violent events in the universe. Shortly after a distant star exploded in a bright **supernova** in 1987, the International Ultraviolet Explorer identified a shock wave of hot gas around the explosion. UV telescopes can observe supernova remnants such as **neutron stars** that give off little **visible light.** Such telescopes also observe young, bright stars that shine in ultraviolet. UV telescopes have even observed the two stars in **binary star** systems ripping gas from each other.

INTERGALACTIC GAS

UV telescopes have also been used to identify the **chemical elements** in gas found in deep space. Such observations rely on intense light from distant **galaxies** to illuminate the gas. The Far Ultraviolet Spectroscopic Explorer (FUSE) was launched in 1999. It discovered an extremely hot, thin cloud of gas that surrounds our galaxy. This gas may reach as far as our nearest galactic neighbors. Such gas may offer clues to how the massive **black holes** in the cores of galaxies influence the formation of stars.

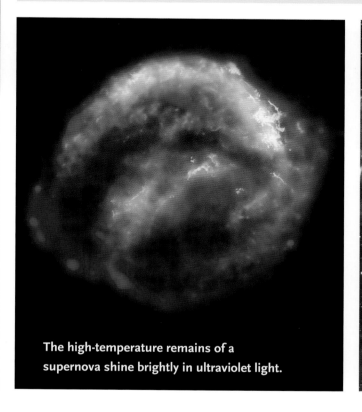

The high-temperature remains of a supernova shine brightly in ultraviolet light.

The star AE Aurigae illuminates a great cloud of carbon dust in an ultraviolet image from NASA's Far Ultraviolet Spectroscopic Explorer satellite.

HOW DOES AN X-RAY TELESCOPE WORK?

Beyond **ultraviolet light** is **electromagnetic radiation** with even shorter **wavelengths.** Scientists call this high-energy light **X rays.** X rays have so much energy that they can pass through many kinds of materials. For example, X rays can pass through the soft tissues of your body. In contrast, bones, teeth, and other hard parts of the body absorb X rays. Physicians use X rays to see these parts. Astronomers use X rays to study such exotic objects as **neutron stars** and **black holes.**

DID YOU KNOW?

The German physicist Wilhelm C. Roentgen discovered X rays in 1895. He called them X rays because at first he did not understand what they were. "X" is a scientific symbol for the unknown.

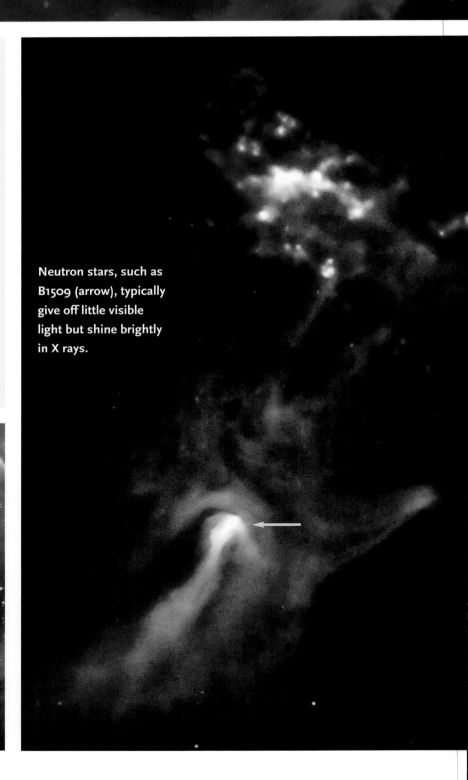

Neutron stars, such as B1509 (arrow), typically give off little visible light but shine brightly in X rays.

MIRROR, MIRROR

The high energy of X rays presents challenges to building an X-ray telescope. Like extreme ultraviolet waves, X rays can be reflected off a mirror only at a small angle by using **grazing incidence mirrors.**

For example, the XMM-Newton was launched by the European Space Agency in 1999. It has three X-ray telescopes that work together. Each telescope is made of 58 mirrored tubes nested inside each other. The mirrors focus X rays onto a **charge-coupled device (CCD).** XMM-Newton also has a **spectrometer** for analyzing the **spectrum** of incoming X rays.

The Chandra X-ray Observatory was launched by NASA in 1999. Its **resolution** is equivalent to the ability to read a stop sign from a distance of 12 miles (20 kilometers). Like the XMM-Newton, Chandra uses mirrored tubes to focus X rays onto a CCD.

LEAD SLATS

Some X-ray telescopes have no mirror. Instead, they use iron or lead slats to block all X rays except those from one area. Light entering the telescope goes to a detector filled with a gas that absorbs X rays. An electronic device inside the detector counts the number of times the X rays interact with the gas. Such devices are used to detect X rays that are too energetic to be reflected even by grazing incidence mirrors.

The XMM-Newton houses three X-ray telescopes, each made up of 58 mirrored tubes nested inside each other.

A SUPERNOVA'S REMAINS

X-ray telescopes are ideal for observing such violent events as **supernovae**. When a dying **star** collapses, a powerful shock wave rips through its outer atmosphere, heating it to millions of degrees. Gases heated to such extreme temperatures shine brightly in X rays.

X-ray telescopes have also observed the hot core the supernova leaves behind. For example, in A.D. 1054, a supernova lighted the skies for weeks. Today, X-ray telescopes can observe a hot **neutron star** where the supernova occurred.

BINARY BLACK HOLES

X-ray telescopes have produced some of the best evidence for the existence of **black holes.** Some black holes occur in **binary star** systems (two-star systems). Black holes in such systems often steal gas from the companion star. This gas becomes very hot as it falls into the black hole, causing the gas to shine brightly in X rays. For example, Cygnus X-1 is one of the brightest sources of X rays in the sky. Cygnus X-1 is a binary star, with a supergiant blue star circling around a compact, invisible companion. This companion is smaller than Earth's moon but has 10 times as much **mass** as our sun. (Mass is the amount of matter in an object.) Most scientists believe the companion can only be a black hole.

SUPERMASSIVE BLACK HOLES

The Chandra X-ray Observatory has produced evidence that tens of millions of galaxies have a supermassive black hole at their center. These black holes are far larger than Cygnus X-1. For example, at the center of our galaxy, a supermassive black hole called Sagittarius A* has a mass about 4 million times as great as the mass of the sun.

A long, powerful jet of gas from the core of the galaxy Centaurus A shines in X rays. The X rays come from gases heated to millions of degrees by a supermassive black hole.

X-ray telescopes have made important discoveries about the hottest objects in the universe, including supernovae and black holes.

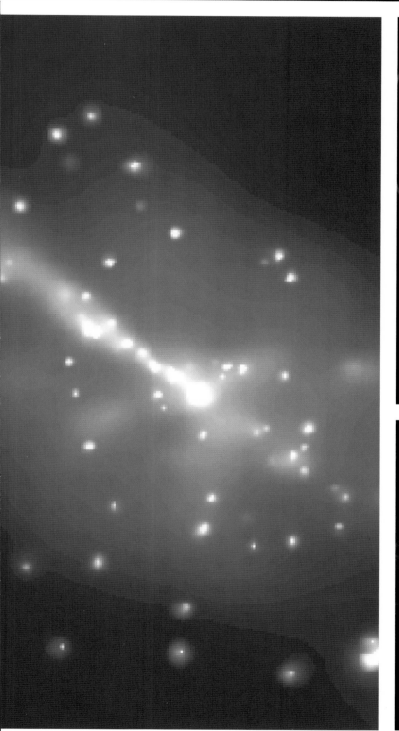

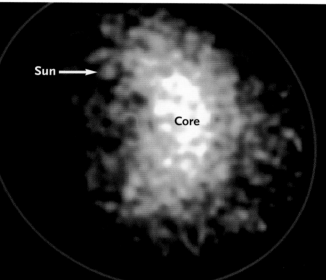

The discovery that a comet, Comet Hyakutake (above), shines with X rays surprised scientists studying Hyakutake's path across Earth's skies. Astronomers speculated that heated gas on the sunlit side of the comet emitted the X rays.

The *binary* (two-star) system known as Cygnus X-1 glows brightly with X rays, as a black hole consumes hot gas from a companion blue supergiant star.

GAMMA-RAY DETECTORS

Gamma rays have the shortest **wavelength** and the highest energy of any type of **electromagnetic radiation.** Gamma rays are billions of times more energetic than the **visible light** we can see with our eyes. In fact, they are so energetic that no kind of mirror can reflect them. To observe gamma rays, **observatories** carry devices called **scintillators.** When gamma rays strike an atom, a shower of particles and radiation is released. In a scintillator, the shower sets off a flash of light that allows astronomers to observe the gamma rays indirectly.

GAMMA-RAY BURSTS

Like **ultraviolet light** and **X rays,** gamma rays are blocked by the Earth's atmosphere. When scientists began to make gamma-ray observations above the atmosphere in the 1960's, they discovered extremely bright flashes of gamma rays from distant galaxies. Such a flash is called a **gamma-ray burst (GRB).** In order to learn more about GRB's, astronomers have launched a series of increasingly sophisticated observatories.

FROM COMPTON TO FERMI

In 1991, NASA launched the Compton Gamma Ray Observatory. The Compton mapped sources of gamma rays throughout the universe, observing thousands of GRB's.

The moon gives off gamma rays as it is struck by high-energy particles that come from deep space.

DID YOU KNOW?

In 1997, two orbiting telescopes detected a gamma-ray burst that was briefly brighter than all the rest of the universe.

In 2004, astronomers launched an observatory called the Swift Gamma-Ray Burst Mission. Swift uses a wide-angle telescope to detect gamma-ray bursts. The craft can then turn to point an X-ray telescope and a combined ultraviolet and **optical** telescope at the source of the burst. Swift also alerts astronomers on the ground, so they can quickly focus their telescopes on the GRB.

In 2008, NASA launched the Fermi Gamma-ray Space Telescope, the most powerful gamma-ray observatory ever built. Fermi can survey the entire sky every three hours. A series of sensors placed around the observatory also detect lower-energy gamma rays. Powerful computers process the huge amount of data gathered by the Fermi. Astronomers hope the Fermi can help explain how black holes accelerate immense jets of material to nearly the speed of light. Fermi may also help scientists learn more about the causes of GRB's.

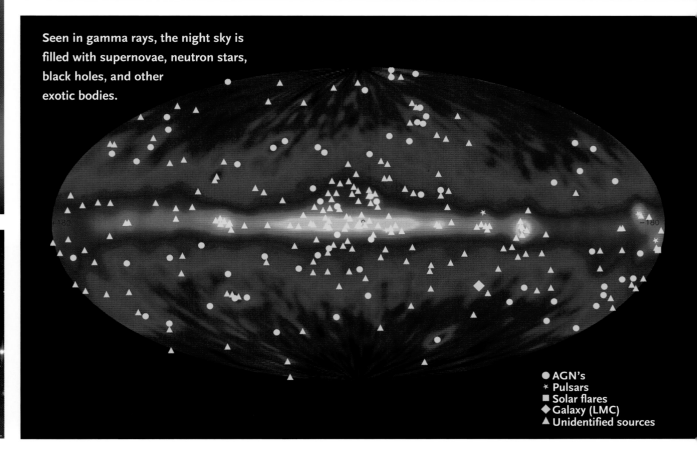

Seen in gamma rays, the night sky is filled with supernovae, neutron stars, black holes, and other exotic bodies.

● AGN's
✳ Pulsars
■ Solar flares
◆ Galaxy (LMC)
▲ Unidentified sources

GAMMA-RAY JETS

Astronomical objects such as **neutron stars** and **black holes** give off **gamma rays.** These objects spin rapidly. As they pull in matter from their surroundings, they may form powerful jets at their poles. Matter is accelerated to extremely high energy in the jets, until it glows with gamma rays.

THE BRIGHTEST FLASH

Gamma-ray bursts (GRB's) are the brightest events in the universe. Most GRB's last for only a few seconds, but the bursts release as much light in those few seconds as the sun would release over 10 billion years. In 1997, two orbiting telescopes detected a burst in a **galaxy** 12 billion **light-years** away that was briefly brighter than all the rest of the universe. In 2008, the Fermi observed a burst that was even brighter. GRB's are also extremely rare. Astronomers observe only about one a day from the entire universe.

Astronomers classify GRB's as either long or short. Long GRB's are associated with the collapse of **stars.** Short GRB's are associated with the collision of neutron stars or black holes.

WHEN GIANTS COLLAPSE

Scientists believe that most GRB's are caused by collapsing stars. When a star much larger than the sun runs out of fuel, it explodes in a violent **supernova.** After the supernova, the core of the star consumes itself and becomes a black hole. Long GRB's record the death of the core and the birth of a black hole.

WHEN MONSTERS COMBINE

Astronomers believe that short GRB's occur when neutron stars or black holes collide and merge to form a single black hole. When black holes merge, tremendous amounts of energy are released in less than two seconds.

DID YOU KNOW?

A massive star may explode in a supernova after it uses up all its fuel. When the star is unable to sustain nuclear fusion, the star's intense gravity causes it to collapse inward. When the core of the star collapses to about 6 miles (10 kilometers) across, it explodes with tremendous violence, shining as bright as an entire galaxy.

Scientists have discovered that gamma-ray bursts are created by some of the most violent events in the universe.

A neutron star has been captured by the gravitational pull of a black hole (1) in an artist's illustration. As the neutron star spirals inward, powerful waves of gravity ripple out from the orbiting bodies (2). In the final two seconds, the collision produces a gamma-ray burst as bright as an entire galaxy (3). As suddenly as it appeared, the gamma-ray burst disappears, leaving a more massive black hole behind (4).

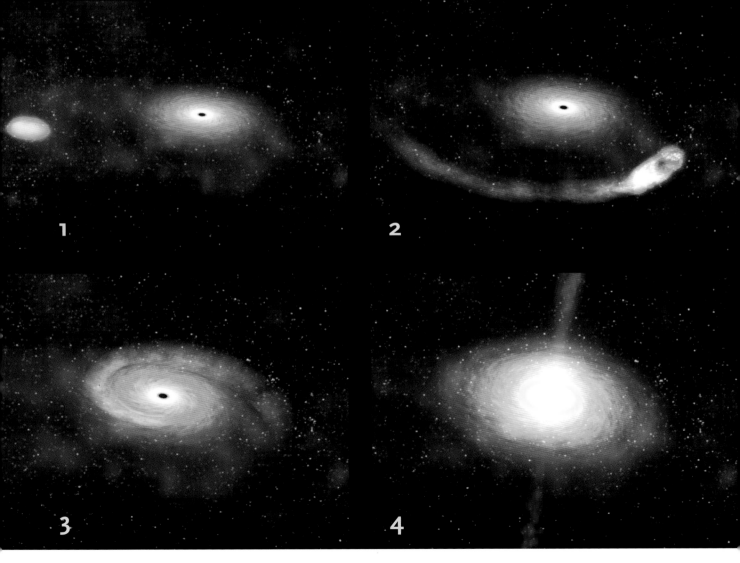

1

2

3

4

Orbiting **observatories** have produced remarkable images of deep space. The Hubble Space Telescope has produced images that show thousands of **galaxies** in only one tiny section of sky. Although some are relatively close, others are billions of **light-years** away. Light left those distant galaxies when the universe was young, giving us a window into the early life of the universe.

THE DARK AGES

Most scientists believe the universe began about 13.7 billion years ago in a tremendous explosion called the **big bang.** As the universe expanded and cooled, **hydrogen** formed. But hundreds of millions of years passed before the first **stars** formed. This period is known as the dark ages. In 2008, the Hubble and Spitzer telescopes observed light that left a distant galaxy 13 billion years ago. The galaxy is in a firestorm of star birth. These newborn stars may have been among the very first to form.

DID YOU KNOW?

In 2007, scientists discovered a great void that is empty of stars and other matter, stretching nearly 1 billion light-years across.

Great filaments made of galaxies stretch across hundreds of millions of light-years in a computer simulation.

The distribution of galaxies in the universe matches the variations in the cosmic microwave background (CMB) radiation.

DISTANT FURY

Orbiting gamma-ray observatories have also recorded light from the depths of space. **Gamma-ray bursts** are so bright that they shine across billions of **light-years.** In 2009, the Swift observatory recorded a burst created when one of the first stars collapsed into a **black hole.** At that time, the universe was only 630 million years old.

GALACTIC FILAMENTS

Orbiting observatories that measure the **cosmic microwave background (CMB)** **radiation** give astronomers another way to explore deep space. Tiny variations in the CMB correspond to the largest structures in the universe. Astronomers have found that galaxies form vast walls and filaments. These structures surround vast empty regions measuring hundreds of millions of light-years across. Orbiting observatories such as the Planck Mission give astronomers a way to observe the universe as a whole, spanning billions of light-years.

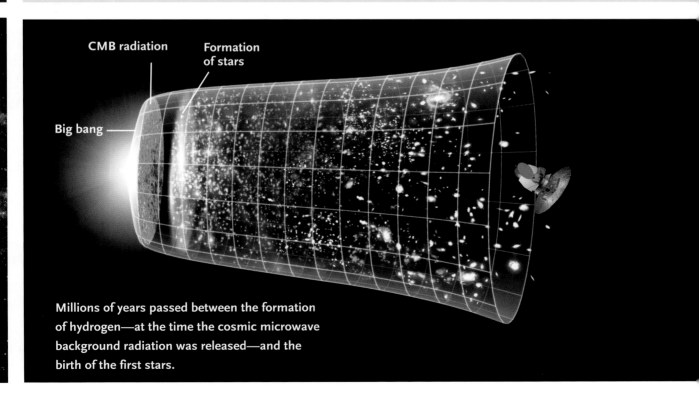

CMB radiation

Formation of stars

Big bang

Millions of years passed between the formation of hydrogen—at the time the cosmic microwave background radiation was released—and the birth of the first stars.

Green areas of a composite image of North America taken by the Terra satellite show where plants are growing the fastest over eight days of spring.

Orbiting **observatories** have not only revolutionized astronomy but also transformed our study of Earth. Weather satellites warn us of approaching storms, and other satellites map the land and the oceans.

WEATHER SATELLITES

Some of the first satellites launched into space were weather satellites. The first successful weather satellite was TIROS, launched by NASA in 1960. Today, many weather satellites observe the Earth. These satellites are equipped with cameras to observe cloud cover and to track storms. Sensors also measure temperature and water vapor.

CLIMATE SATELLITES

Other satellites measure long-term changes in climate. For example, the Ice, Cloud, and land Elevation Satellite (ICEsat), launched in 2003, uses lasers to measure the extent of Arctic sea ice, which is thinning as the world warms. The

NASA's Aura observatory measures changes in the ozone layer, a part of the atmosphere that protects Earth from damaging **ultraviolet light.**

The Terra spacecraft, launched in 1999, helps scientists to study climate change. Among other measurements, it records changes in the atmosphere's temperature.

LAY OF THE LAND

One of the most important Earth-observing programs was Landsat, a series of seven satellites launched from 1972 to 1999. These satellites produced millions of images, surveying our planet in detail. Landsat enabled scientists to better track such changes as the destruction of forests. Today, dozens of satellites provide detailed maps of most areas of our **planet's** surface. Such images are available free of charge on the Internet.

The Laser Geodynamics Satellites measure movements in Earth's crust. Beams from lasers on the surface bounce off reflectors on the satellites. The beams enable scientists to obtain precise measurements of even slight movements of the land.

MOTION OF THE OCEAN

A number of satellites observe the oceans, including NASA's powerful Aqua observatory. In 2008, the United States and France launched the Ocean Surface Topography Mission-Jason 2. This observatory was designed to study the height of the ocean surface and how it is related to climate.

Wildfires and plumes of smoke affecting an area around Denver, Colorado, are tracked in an animation based on data from the Terra satellite.

Tiny, windblown particles called aerosols pass over Africa in an animated image based on data recorded by the Ice, Cloud, and land Elevation Satellite.

Scientists have made many discoveries about the atmosphere of the sun using orbiting **observatories.** These observatories also track the progress of solar storms and can warn scientists if particularly violent storms threaten to cause disruptions on Earth.

THE UNEXPLORED ULTRAVIOLET

Because the atmosphere blocks most **ultraviolet light** and **X rays,** scientists were not able to continually observe these **wavelengths** until they launched orbiting observatories. In the 1970's, NASA used ultraviolet telescopes aboard the Skylab space station to map the sun's outer atmosphere. Skylab observed solar flares and other solar storms.

SOLAR STORMS

The sun goes through long cycles of solar storms that can affect communication equipment and other electronics on Earth. Severe solar storms can damage satellites,

The sun is partly eclipsed by the moon in an image from Japan's Hinode satellite, which studies the sun's magnetic fields and atmosphere.

DID YOU KNOW?

The sun is so large that it would take 1 million Earths, packed together like marbles in a bowl, to fill the space occupied by the sun.

disrupt radio transmissions, and even interfere with the flow of electricity in power lines on Earth. The damage caused by such storms can be reduced with early warning from the orbiting observatories that study the sun.

SOLAR PIONEERS

Scientists have launched a number of solar observatories. The Ulysses observatory, launched in 1990, became the first probe to orbit the sun from pole to pole. It carried X-ray and **gamma-ray** telescopes. In 1995, the European Space Agency (ESA) and NASA launched the Solar and Heliosphere Observatory (SOHO), which gathers information about the sun's interior and outer atmosphere. In 1998, NASA launched the TRACE Observatory to make high-resolution ultraviolet observations of the sun's atmosphere. In 2001, the Genesis spacecraft set out to gather samples of the particles blasted away from the sun.

The latest solar observatory is Hinode, which was launched by Japan in 2006. Hinode studies the sun's magnetic fields, which play an important role in solar storms. Hinode also observes ultraviolet light and X rays from the sun's outer atmosphere.

Hotter gases rise to the surface (light areas) and cooler gases return to the interior (dark areas) in a highly magnified image of the sun's lower atmosphere from the Hinode satellite.

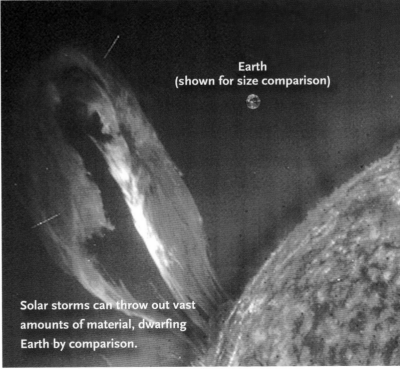

Earth
(shown for size comparison)

Solar storms can throw out vast amounts of material, dwarfing Earth by comparison.

CAN ORBITING OBSERVATORIES BE USED TO SEARCH FOR EXTRASOLAR PLANETS?

Kepler search space
3,000 light-years

Sagittarius Arm

Sun

Orion
Spur

Astronomers have long suspected that **planets** orbit around other **stars,** but they have only found evidence for such **exoplanets** since the early 1990's. Astronomers have found more than 400 exoplanets so far.

METHODS OF DETECTION

Finding exoplanets is difficult. Planets reflect light from the stars they orbit, but a planet's reflected light is easily lost in the brilliance of its parent star. Exoplanets typically have less than one-millionth of their star's brightness.

Most exoplanets have been observed indirectly, through careful measurements of a star's motion. Although a planet is much smaller than a star, its *mass* (amount of matter) is sufficient to tug at the star.

Another method astronomers use to find exoplanets is to measure the slight dimming of a distant star as a planet passes in front of it. Finally, a small number of exoplanets have been detected directly, through observing their reflected light.

At least four planets orbit the star Gliese 581, which is about 20 light-years from Earth.

PLANET HUNTERS

Space-based telescopes have made many exciting contributions to the hunt for exoplanets. The Spitzer Space Telescope produced the first **spectrum** of an exoplanet's light in 2007. The spectrum confirmed the presence of water vapor in the planet's atmosphere. This finding excites scientists because all life on Earth depends upon water. Scientists hope that by searching for planets with water of their own, we may one day discover alien life. In 2008, the Hubble made the first direct observations of an exoplanet in **visible light.** The planet orbits a star called Fomalhaut that is about 25 **light-years** from the Earth.

In 2009, the space-based Kepler Mission began its search for rocky planets similar to Earth. Kepler detects these planets by measuring the slight dimming of the parent star as the planet passes in front of it. To improve its chances of finding exoplanets, Kepler monitors 100,000 stars simultaneously.

Orbiting the star Gliese 581 is a rocky planet with five times as much mass as the Earth, shown in an artist's illustration.

JAMES WEBB

NASA planned to launch the James Webb Space Telescope in 2014. The Webb will carry a mirror about 21 feet (6.5 meters) across, much larger than Hubble's 8-foot (2.4-meter) mirror. The Webb is designed to detect the formation of the first **galaxies** more than 13 billion years ago. Light that has crossed 13 billion **light-years** shows great **redshift** from the expansion of the universe, so the Webb will observe **infrared light**. The **observatory** will orbit more than 900,000 miles (1.5 million kilometers) from Earth, using the planet to block light from the sun.

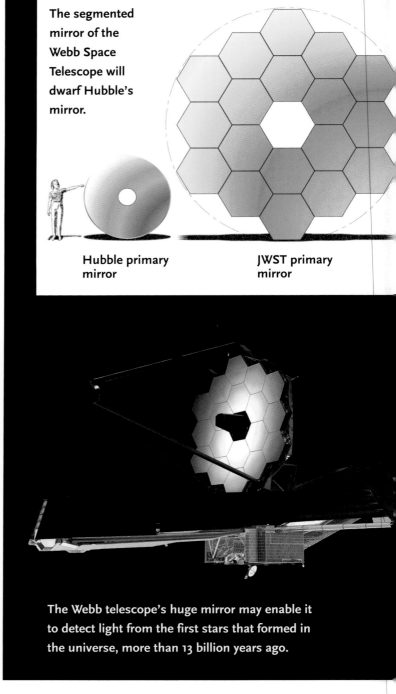

The segmented mirror of the Webb Space Telescope will dwarf Hubble's mirror.

Hubble primary mirror

JWST primary mirror

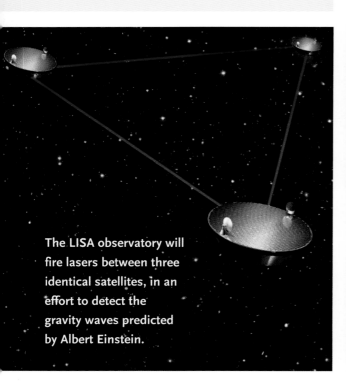

The LISA observatory will fire lasers between three identical satellites, in an effort to detect the gravity waves predicted by Albert Einstein.

The Webb telescope's huge mirror may enable it to detect light from the first stars that formed in the universe, more than 13 billion years ago.

MAKING WAVES

Other space observatories will explore exotic new territory. Physicist Albert Einstein's general theory of relativity predicts that gravitational waves must ripple through space. But scientists have never observed these waves directly. The Laser Interferometer Space Antenna (LISA) observatory will try to detect these waves by firing lasers between three identical satellites spread out over an area larger than the orbit of the moon. Observations of gravitational waves may offer new insights into the formation and behavior of **neutron stars, black holes,** and **supernovae.** LISA could be launched as early as 2018.

MEASURE FOR MEASURE

Another new observatory promises to measure the distance to stars with unprecedented accuracy. The SIM Lite Astrometric Observatory will combine light from two telescopes to produce images with extraordinary sharpness. In addition to measuring distance, SIM Lite will search for Earth-sized **exoplanets** around 250 nearby stars. It could launch as early as 2015.

The SIM Lite Astrometric Observatory will measure the distance to stars with unprecedented accuracy.

GLOSSARY

Asteroid – A small, rocky body orbiting around a star.

Atmospheric distortion – The tendency of pockets of moving air and water vapor in Earth's atmosphere to act like lenses, bending light as it travels to the ground. Atmospheric distortion can make objects viewed through a telescope appear blurry.

Big bang – The cosmic explosion that began the expansion of the universe.

Binary stars – Stars that orbit each other.

Black hole – The collapsed core of a massive star. The gravity of a black hole is so strong that not even light can escape.

Charge-coupled device (CCD) – A computer chip used to record light.

Chemical element – Any substance that contains only one kind of atom. Hydrogen and helium are both chemical elements.

Comet – A small, icy body orbiting a star.

Corona – The outermost layer of the sun's atmosphere.

Cosmic microwave background (CMB) radiation – The most ancient electromagnetic radiation in the universe. Variations in the CMB correspond to the distribution of galaxies in the universe.

Doppler effect – The change in wavelength of light or sound caused by the relative motion of the source and the observer.

Electromagnetic radiation – Any form of light, ranging from radio waves, to microwaves, to infrared light, to visible light, to ultraviolet light, to X rays, to gamma rays.

Exoplanet – Any planet in orbit around a star other than the sun.

Galaxy – A vast system of stars, gas, dust, and other matter held together in space by mutual gravitational attraction.

Gamma-ray burst (GRB) – An extremely bright flash of gamma rays from a distant galaxy.

Gamma rays – The form of light with the shortest wavelengths. Gamma rays are invisible to the unaided eye.

Gravity – The force of attraction that acts between all objects because of their mass.

Grazing incidence mirrors – Mirrors arranged so that high-energy electromagnetic radiation will graze the surface of the mirrors to come into focus. Some grazing incidence mirrors are nested inside each other like tubes in an oil drum.

Hydrogen – The simplest chemical element. Hydrogen is the most abundant substance in the universe. It fuels most stars.

Infrared light – A form of light with long wavelengths. Also called heat radiation. Infrared is invisible to the unaided eye.

Lens – A curved piece of glass or other material that gathers and focuses light.

Light-year – The distance light travels in a vacuum in one year. One light-year is equal to 5.88 trillion miles (9.46 trillion kilometers).

Mass – The amount of matter in an object.

Microwaves – A kind of radio wave with relatively short wavelengths. Microwaves are invisible to the unaided eye.

Nebula — A cloud of dust and gas in space.

Neutron star — A star that has collapsed into a small area with extremely high mass. Neutron stars form from the remains of massive stars that have exploded in supernovae.

Objective — The large mirror or lens in a telescope that gathers light.

Observatory — A structure used to observe the heavens.

Optical — Of or relating to visible light.

Payload — The scientific instruments or other cargo carried by a rocket.

Planet — A large, round heavenly body that orbits a star.

Pulsar — A neutron star that gives off regular pulses of electromagnetic radiation.

Radio waves — The form of light with the longest wavelengths. Radio waves are invisible to the unaided eye.

Redshift — A shift in light's wavelength toward longer, redder wavelengths. Doppler redshift is caused by the Doppler effect. Cosmological redshift is caused by the expansion of the universe.

Resolution — The amount of light a telescope gathers. Resolution determines how clear an image will be.

Scintillator — A device used to observe gamma rays. It measures the flash of light given off when gamma rays strike an atom, releasing a shower of particles and radiation.

Solar panel — A device that converts sunlight into electrical energy.

Solar system — The planetary system that includes the sun and Earth.

Sounding rocket — A relatively small rocket used to carry scientific instruments into low orbit.

Spectrometer — An instrument that divides light into its spectrum for analysis.

Spectrum, spectra — Light divided into its different wavelengths. A spectrum may provide astronomers with information about a heavenly body's chemical composition, motion, and distance.

Star — A huge, shining ball in space that produces a tremendous amount of light and other forms of energy.

Supernova, supernovae — An exploding star that can become billions of times as bright as the sun before gradually fading from view. A supernova occurs when a massive star uses up all its fuel.

Ultraviolet light — A form of light with short wavelengths. Ultraviolet light is invisible to the unaided eye.

Visible light — The form of light human beings can see with their eyes.

X rays — A form of light with short wavelengths. X rays are invisible to the unaided eye.

Wavelength — The distance between successive crests, or peaks, of a wave. Wavelength is used to distinguish among different forms of light. Radio waves have the longest wavelengths, and gamma rays have the shortest.

FOR MORE INFORMATION

WEB SITES

HubbleSite

http://hubblesite.org

NASA's comprehensive Web site about the Hubble Telescope includes basic facts, news stories, Hubble photographs, and resources for students.

NASA Science: Missions

http://nasascience.nasa.gov/missions

Find out about every space mission NASA has sponsored in the past, is currently conducting, and plans to develop.

National Radio Astronomy Observatory

http://www.nrao.edu

The National Science Foundation has created this Web site to help viewers understand radio astronomy.

Spitzer Space Telescope

http://www.spitzer.caltech.edu

Learn about the Spitzer mission, how its infrared telescope works, and what it is teaching astronomers.

BOOKS

Death Stars, Weird Galaxies, and a Quasar-Spangled Universe by Karen Taschek (University of New Mexico Press, 2006)

The Hubble Space Telescope by Margaret W. Carruthers (Franklin Watts, 2003)

Spacecraft for Astronomy by Joseph A. Angelo (Facts on File, 2007)

Star Spotters: Telescopes and Observatories by David Jefferis (Crabtree Publishing, 2009)

INDEX

atmospheric distortion, 4, 6-7

big bang, 27, 33, 50
black holes, 41, 42, 44, 47, 48, 51
blueshift, 24

charge-coupled devices (CCD's), 22, 29, 35, 43
climate studies, 52-53
comets, 14; Hyakutake, 45
cosmic microwave background (CMB) radiation, 32, 33, 51

Einstein, Albert, 58, 59
electromagnetic radiation, 6, 24-25
elements, chemical, 26
European Space Agency (ESA), 35, 43, 55

galaxies, 27, 29; Andromeda, 36-37; birth of, 50-51, 58; gamma-ray bursts in, 48; in gas, 41; M33, 50; Milky Way, 35, 36
gamma-ray bursts (GRB's), 46-49, 51
gamma rays, 25, 46-49
gas, intergalactic, 41
Geiger counters, 13
gravitational waves, 59
gravity, 16, 20, 38, 48-49

Hubble Space Telescope, 4-5, 28-29, 38, 57, 58; data transmission by, 17, 23; images from, 30-31, 50; launching, 20, 21
hydrogen, 26, 50, 51

infrared light, 7, 10, 11, 17, 25, 31, 34-37

life, 57
light, 6-7, 22, 24-27

Mars, 15
microwaves, 25, 32, 33
mirrors, 28, 38; grazing incidence, 39, 43
moon, 14, 54

National Aeronautics and Space Administration (NASA), 10-11. See also observatories, orbiting; rockets; space probes
nebulae, 7, 30, 36; Eskimo, 4; Helix, 34
Newton, Sir Isaac, 26

observatories: balloon, 6, 8-9; ground-based, 6, 16
observatories, airborne, 6, 10-11; Galileo, 10; Kuiper Airborne Observatory, 10, 11, 26; Stratospheric Observatory for Infrared Astronomy (SOFIA), 11
observatories, orbiting, 4, 16-17; deep space studies by, 50-51; Earth studies by, 52-53; extrasolar planet studies by, 56-57; first, 18-19; future, 58-59; launching, 20-21; parts of, 22-23; solar studies by, 54-55
observatories, orbiting, names of: Aqua, 53; Ariel, 18; Aura, 52-53; Chandra X-ray Observatory, 43, 44; Compton Gamma Ray Observatory, 20, 46; Cosmic Background Explorer (CBE), 33; Einstein Observatory (HEAO 2), 19; Explorer 1, 18, 20; Extreme Ultraviolet Explorer, 39; Far Ultraviolet Spectrographic Explorer, 41; Fermi Gamma-ray Space Telescope, 17, 47, 48; Genesis, 55; Herschel Space Observatory, 16, 17, 22, 35; High Energy Astronomy Observatory (HEAO), 19; Hinode, 40, 54, 55; Ice, Cloud, and land Elevation Satellite, 52, 53; Infrared Astronomical Satellite, 35; James Webb Space Telescope, 58; Kepler Mission, 17, 56, 57; LAGEOS, 53; Landsat, 53; Laser Interferometer Space Antenna (LISA), 58, 59; Ocean Surface Topography Mission-Jason 2, 53; Orbiting Astronomical Observatory-2, 19; Planck Space Observatory, 33, 51; SIM Lite Astrometric Observatory, 59; Skylab, 54; Solar and Heliospheric Observatory (SOHO), 55; Spitzer Space Telescope, 7, 34, 35, 50, 57; Sputnik 1, 18; Swift Gamma Ray Burst Mission, 47, 51; Terra, 53; TIROS, 52; TRACE, 55; Ulysses, 55; Wilkinson Microwave Anisotropy Probe (WMAP), 32, 33; XMM Newton, 43. See also Hubble Space Telescope
oceans, 53
orbits, 16-17

payloads, 12, 20
planets, 14; extrasolar (exoplanets), 36, 56-57, 59

radio waves, 24, 25, 32-33
redshift, 24, 27, 36, 58
resolution, 32
rockets: Ares V, 21; Black Brandt, 12; Jupiter C, 20; launching observatories, 16, 20-21; Orion, 13; Saturn V, 21; sounding, 12-13
Roentgen, Wilhelm C., 42

Sagittarius A*, 41
satellite observatories. See observatories, orbiting
Saturn, 15, 31
scintillators, 46
solar panels, 22, 23, 29
solar storms, 40, 54-55
space probes, 14-15; atmospheric, 15; Huygens, 14, 15; lander, 15; Mars Reconnaissance Orbiter, 14; Venus Express, 15
spectra, 24-27, 39, 57
spectrographs, 29, 39
spectrometers, 22, 26
stars, 30, 31, 36-37; binary, 41, 44; birth of, 50-51; exoplanets of, 56-57; motions of, 24, 26-27; neutron, 41, 42, 44, 48; spectra of, 24, 26, 27; twinkling by, 6
stars, names of: AE Aurigae, 41; Cygnus X-1, 44, 45; Eta Carinae, 27; Gliese 581, 56, 57
sun, 6, 40, 54-55; corona of, 40
supernovae, 19, 41, 44, 48

telescopes, 22; gamma-ray, 46-49; infrared, 10, 11, 34-37; radio, 32-33; ultraviolet, 38-41, 54; X-ray, 42-45. See also observatories, orbiting
Titan, 14, 15

ultraviolet (UV) light, 17, 19, 25, 30, 38-41, 53, 54
universe, 27, 33, 50-51

Venus, 15

water, 57
wavelength, 24-25
weather satellites, 52

X rays, 13, 19, 25, 42-45, 54

ACKNOWLEDGMENTS

The publishers acknowledge the following sources for illustrations. Credits read from top to bottom, left to right, on their respective pages. All illustrations, maps, charts, and diagrams were prepared by the staff unless otherwise noted.

Cover: European Space Agency

1　NASA

4-5　NASA; NASA, Andrew Fruchter and the ERO Team; Sylvia Baggett (STScI), Richard Hook (ST-ECF), Zoltan Levay (STScI)

6-7　WORLD BOOK illustrations by Matt Carrington; NASA/JPL-Caltech/E. Churchwell (Univ. of Wisconsin)

8-9　© Guy Clavel, AFP/Getty Images; © Peter Barthol, EPA/ZUMA Press; © Yuri Mashkov, Itar-Tass/Landov; WORLD BOOK illustration

10-11　NASA Ames Photo/Eric James; NASA; NASA

12-13　NASA; AP Photo; NASA/MSFC

14-15　NASA/JPL; ESA; ESA

16-17　ESA and the SPIRE consortium; © Ball Aerospace; NASA/JPL-Caltech; ESA and the SPIRE Consortium; ESA/AOES Medialab; background: Hubble Space Telescope image (NASA/ESA/STScI)

18-19　AP Photo; WORLD BOOK illustration; NASA; NASA

20-21　NASA; NASA/Sandra Joseph and Kevin O'Connell; NASA; NASA/ESA

22-23　ESA; NASA

24-25　ESA and the PACS Consortium; WORLD BOOK illustrations by Ernest Norcia; WORLD BOOK illustrations

26-27　© North Wind Picture Archives/Alamy Images; National Institute of Standards and Technology; NASA, ESA, and the Hubble SM4 ERO Team

28-29　NASA

30-31　NASA, ESA, and the Hubble SM4 ERO Team; Science Team, and ESA; NASA, H. Ford (JHU), G. Illingworth (UCSC/LO), M. Clampin (STScI), G. Hartig (STScI), the ACS Science Team, and ESA; NASA and E. Karkoschka (Univ. of Arizona); NASA, ESA, and R. Thompson/Univ. Arizona

32-33　NASA/WMAP Science Team; NASA; ESA, LFI & HFI Consortia (Planck), Background image: Axel Mellinger

34-35　NASA/JPL-Caltech/J. Hora (Harvard-Smithsonian CfA); NASA/JPL-Caltech/Univ. of Wisconsin

36-37　NASA/JPL-Caltech/K. Gordon (Univ. of Arizona); © Scientifica/Visuals Unlimited/Getty Images; NASA/JPL Caltech/UIUC & Caltech/AURA

38-39　© Edward Kinsman, Photo Researchers; © Edward Kinsman, Photo Researchers; NASA-JSC

40-41　NASA/JPL; NASA/ESA/JHU/R. Sankrit & W. Blair; T. A. Rector and B. A. Wolpa, NOAO, AURA and NSF

42-43　NASA/CXC/SAO/P. Slane; ESA/D. Ducros

44-45　NASA/SAO/R. Kraft; NASA/GSFC/MPE, C. Lisse, M. Mumma, K Dennerl, J. Schmitt, J. Englhauser; NASA/CXC/SAO

46-47　NASA/GSFC, D. J. Thompson, D. L. Bertsch; NASA/GSFC/USRA, D. J. Morris (UNH), R. Mukherjee

48-49　NASA/Dana Berry

50-51　Max Planck Institute; NASA/JPL-Caltech/Univ. of Arizona; NASA/WMAP Science Team

52-53　NASA/GSFS, MODIS Instrument Team; NASA/GSFS, Scientific Visualization Studio

54-55　NASA/JAXA; NASA/JAXA/PPARC; NASA/ESA

56-57　NASA/Kepler Mission/Jon Lomberg; Digital Sky Survey; ESO

58-59　NASA; NASA/ESA; NASA; NASA